MW00720772

Christmas Letter 2011

We hiked in wildflowers and on
mountain vistas in Oregon and Washington
Looked for tiny seashells in Kaui. We've Experienced
went for long walks with friends the sister's
became a grand Uncle and Auntie Quilt
Trekked up Lombard Street and saw the Show
Giants loso.

We worked hard and

Marveled at the sandcastles on a
wet, and cold, and foggy Cannon
Beach Day. Oh, and we worked
And we hope to do it over and over
again.
Merry Christmas.

Love — Michael, Ellen and Harper